MARGUERITE DE NAVARRE

MARGUERITE DE NAVARRE

A Literary Queen

Rouben Cholakian

To order additional copies of this book, contact:
Xlibris
1-888-795-4274
www.Xlibris.com
Orders@Xlibris.com
746874

CONTENTS

I

The Political Figure

II

The Writer

III

Legacy

For
Kathryn

I

The Political Figure

At about the same time that Christopher Columbus set out to discover the world, a noteworthy princess and queen was born –"noteworthy," not only because she was a queen, but because she was a queen who wrote books. There are not many royal lives that turn out to be literary ones as well. That is why this particular royal life is so fascinating.

THE COURT

Although born into the poor side of the royal family, Marguerite de Navarre never knew anything but court life. She was born on April 12, 1492 at the minor court at Romorantin. Two years later, the family moved to her father, Charles's other court in Cognac. It was here that Marguerite's younger brother François was born, a fact that made the king, Louis XII, very uneasy since he had not yet produced a male heir.

From that moment, for all intents and purposes, the Angoulême family lived under house arrest. When in 1515 Louis XII died without producing a successor, against all odds, François mounted the French throne. Rejoicing, the Angoulêmes moved from their own court to the royal one at Amboise. The new king was twenty-five, his delighted sister Marguerite was twenty-seven, and together they were to change the world.

They were fully prepared to do so because of a powerful, single-minded, and intelligent mother who had carefully nurtured them in court manners and book learning. In many ways, Louise de Savoie is the real heroine of this story. She was by any standards, of any age, a remarkable woman. She endured the humiliation of her husband's live-in mistress, Antoinette de Polignac. She bore the mortifying and shameful interferences into her private life of the king's peering spy, Gié. But most significantly, she defied the conventions of the time by insisting that both of her children receive a thorough education in language and literature. In good measure,

Marguerite became the intellectual and writing queen we now admire because of this strong-willed woman.

There was already an intellectual tradition to fall back on. Louise had inherited from her husband's side an impressive library of manuscripts and books which she encouraged her children to read, most particularly her daughter who shared her mother's love of books.

It is no wonder therefore that when François became his country's monarch, he quickly transformed his predecessor's dull and uninspired court into one of the most brilliant and active of the century. And surely one of the brightest stars in that new artistic constellation was the king's clever and quick-witted older sibling, Marguerite.

She was not just an entertaining and colorful presence. She was a true participant in the royal court life, in both its pleasures as well as its intrigues.

The king valued his sister's diplomatic skills and often turned to her for advice and counsel. Many of the foreign ambassadors who visited the French court remembered her for her political acumen and wise perceptions.

Years later, those skills stood Marguerite in good stead as she effectively negotiated her brother's release from the clutches of his archenemy Charles V. The French army had been decisively defeated at the 1524 battle at Pavia, and François was embarrassingly taken away to Spain as Charles's prisoner. Louise, secure in her daughter's competence, sent Marguerite to Spain to do the bargaining, and everyone came away admiring this adroit young woman who stood her ground.

Marguerite's experiences in her development as a sexual creature were to prove far from positive. She fell in love with one of her brother's closest adolescent companions, the charming and vivacious, Guillaume

Gouffier, Seigneur de Bonnivet. He, however, saw her less as a partner in love than an object to conquer. This much-admired friend took advantage of Marguerite's innocence and tried to seduce her. This experience left her forever traumatized and thus became a central theme in her collection of tales, *L'Heptaméron*.

Women of Marguerite's class were seen as salable commodities, and before long, Marguerite found herself on the marriage block. In one significant respect, a peasant girl was better off than a lady of the court; she could marry for love. From their youngest age, princesses of the court were pawns for the use of men who made territorial conquest through desirable conjugal arrangements.

At one point, it was suggested that Marguerite be married off to the Prince of Wales who was soon to become Henry VIII of England. How different would her story have been if he had not rebuffed her? Like some delicacy at the dinner table, she was then offered to Charles d'Alençon. Such an alliance allowed the king the chance to bring the contested Armagnac land under royal hegemony.

This was not only a totally loveless match but an obvious contradiction of personality traits. She was high-spirited and intelligent while Charles was dull and uninspired.

The damp and dark Normandy castle, which became Marguerite's home for nearly fifteen years, had little to recommend it. Gone suddenly were the exciting political events of François's court, gone the music, dance, and lively conversation which must have so delighted Princess Marguerite who was often the center of attention. Her only consolation was a sweet-natured mother-in-law whose religious fervor was a model to the susceptible young woman in search of compensation and spiritual sustenance.

And yet when Charles fell ill, Marguerite lovingly nursed him until his death in 1526. Years later in one of her autobiographical poems, Marguerite alludes to this first husband with kindness and generosity. There was, however, no issue from this first dreary and loveless marriage.

The second marriage was quite a different story. Henry of Navarre was young (by nearly ten years), handsome, bold, and anything but boring. The attractive couple were conjoined with much pomp and circumstance. The king was happy because once again, he was able to expand his territorial influence. Marguerite herself was pleased because this second husband was like an Adonis next to the first. While it cannot be said that Henry, always a womanizer, was the ideal mate, overall, this was a far more successful liaison, producing two children, a son who died young, and a daughter, Jeanne d'Albret who was to become mother of another French monarch, Henry IV.

THE CHURCH

Marguerite did not live long enough to experience the violent and bloody religious eruption that shook her country during the second half of the century. She did, nevertheless, witness the first rumblings of reform, a struggle that proceeded on two fronts:

(1)   in the increased distribution of scriptural translations prepared by eminent Biblical scholars like Erasmus and Jacques Lefèvre d'Etaples, and

(2)   in the diligent efforts of outspoken critics of the church like Luther, Hus, and Calvin.

It would seem that in the 1520s, Marguerite experienced her own severe spiritual crisis. It may be that she never fully recovered from her attempted rape by Bonnivet, a frightening experience that would haunt her for the rest of her days. Moreover, several important women in her entourage died at about the same time, forcing Marguerite to confront the whole notion of the pain and sorrow of losing people with whom she was intimately connected: the death of her sister-in-law, Claude de France, fragile to begin with, and probably the victim of too many close pregnancies, the death of a favored aunt on her mother's side of the family, Philiberte de Savoie, with whom she had shared many literary interests. But no doubt what pushed her over the edge was the sudden death of one of the king's young daughters, Charlotte. This premature death especially distressed Marguerite who wanted to cling to the idea of a just and loving God. It was one thing to lose people of mature age, quite another that of an innocent young girl who had not yet learned all that there was to learn about life.

In her extreme depression and resulting religious doubts, the princess turned for advice and sustenance to one of the outstanding clerics of her time, Guillaume Briçonnet, Bishop of Meaux. It was a decisive moment, for this Bishop was one of the leading reformists of the time. A rich and fascinating correspondence was established between this intelligent reformist-minded priest and the bewildered and despondent Duchess of Alençon.

The dark emotions had so welled up in the heart of this despairing princess that when Marguerite contacted Briçonnet, it was like the sudden release of a floodgate of repressed feelings. She pleadingly writes: "I turn to you, entreating you to make yourself the means of reaching [God] through prayer." Her letters to him refer to her need for "spiritual succour." In her gloomiest state, she describes herself as "unworthy," "ignorant," and "worse than dead."

The Bishop of Meaux, serving more and more as a father confessor, supported and encouraged his royal supplicant. It has to be said however that when Marguerite's reformist ideas brought about disapproving denunciations from the conservative forces at the Sorbonne—while her brother came to her defence—Briçonnet, fearing for his own safety, took refuge in cautious and obedient silence. His vigilant retreat measures the growing tensions in a Catholic country where liberals had to run for their lives, often quite literally. Marguerite, on the other hand, had protection from on high, a generous brother who wanted to save his sister and his own reputation from disgrace. Highly vulnerable creatures like the good Bishop of Meaux had none.

In spite of this rapidly changing mentality on the religious front, Marguerite persisted in using her influence to support the liberal reformist's cause. She named liberal clerics and protected beleaguered reformists such as the eminent poet, Clément Marot, at one point, a part of her own cultural entourage.

The hostilities came to a head in 1530 when a Protestant leaning cleric, Antoine Marcourt, posted anti-Catholic notices in and around Paris and even near the residence of the king. Marguerite took this as a warning to lay low for a while. She wisely retired to her own lands in the south where she was more or less her own authority. Less preoccupied by the events of the day, this may indeed have been a time when she started to do a good deal more serious writing.

From her correspondence with Briçonnet, Marguerite discovered a newfound peace of mind, an inner spiritual strength that had been seriously lacking in her life up to that point. But she learned something else, that she was a burgeoning writer. *La doulce escripture* ("sweet writing"), as she lovingly came to call it, could bring her solace that she had never known before.

It is said that age reinforces character traits. While François continued his war games, dangerously depleting the national treasury, recklessly womanizing, and thus risking his health, his older sister seemed to have a greater need to withdraw into herself. Several points of conflict, moreover, had put a strain on this otherwise loving family tie.

The king found it harder and harder to come to his sister's support in her reformist leanings. Another terrible estrangement came with the marriageability of Marguerite's only daughter, Jeanne.

François, ever the political strategist, could only see her as a way to realize his territorial ambitions. Just like her mother, she was putty in his royal hands. He recommended a series of matches, first, the Duke de Guise and finally, the German Duke de Clèves.

Marguerite was a princess and a queen, but she was also a mother. Determined to do all that she could to save her only child from a match that pleased an ambitious king but neither a far-too-young daughter nor an angry and protective mother, she unobtrusively warred against the royal will. She soon realized that she had little real influence on a powerful monarch, even if he were an idolized brother. So despite her every effort, in 1541, the disheartened Marguerite had no choice but to give in to the king's wishes.

At an ostentatious wedding ceremony where the entire court had been assembled, the twelve-year-old Jeanne, weeping and heavily laden with jewels and ornaments, had a royal temper tantrum. She absolutely refused to walk down the aisle. Finally, a signal was given and like some weighty inanimate object, she was literally carried toward her future husband by one of the members of the king's entourage. Marguerite was humiliated to say nothing of the poor helpless child who felt she was being taken to her death.

Humiliated but not defeated, Marguerite decided to expend all of her energies to seeing that this insane marriage would never be consummated. We see the canny mother and sister at her most strategically enterprising. She found multiple excuses not to send Jeanne off to join her undesirable and undesired German husband.

In the end, because of non-consummation, Marguerite managed to convince the pope to dissolve this marriage. It was a rare moment in this complicated brother-sister relationship when the wiles of a clever and single-minded woman outsmarted the self-serving determination of a formidable king. It didn't happen often, and Marguerite must have wallowed in the sweet victory of a hard fought battle.

It may well be that their intimacy suffered from these events and the once loving friendship took a turn for the worse. And yet warm memories of good times lingered on in Marguerite's mind, and when, in 1547, she received news that François was gravely ill, despite her own weakened condition, she set out to be by her sibling's bedside. Very tired, she had to stop halfway to catch her breath. It was at the monastery at Tusson that the queen learned that her journey was in vain. She would never reach François; he was already no longer in her world.

What must have gone through his head? Did he die thinking his sister had abandoned him? It was not so. His death unmistakably hastened hers.

Marguerite became a virtual recluse, rarely leaving her estates in the south, Nérac, Pau, and the modest dwelling at Odos which she had only recently acquired.

She spent what little energy she had left in these closing years overseeing the publication of her collected works, her last literary will and testament. She was determined to announce to the world that she had been not only a political figure but a literary one.

By the winter of 1549, drained, exhausted, and moving ever more slowly, Marguerite was finally forced to take to her bed. On December 21, surrounded by only a few friends and staff members, and after three days in which she did not speak a single word, she went to join her brother. The Queen of Navarre was forty-seven.

II

The Writer

Theater

When Marguerite took to writing plays, she was not inventing in a vacuum. The French theater was alive and well, and she inherited from an already old and rich tradition. On into the beginning of the new century—although mainly on the wane—plays in the medieval manner were still around: religiously oriented works like the *Mysteries, Moralities, and Miracles* and secular pieces such as *Farce*s and the *Sotties*.

This was a time of transition, and Marguerite's own contributions reflect those changes. In a sense therefore, it can be said that Marguerite had one foot in the medieval past and one foot clearly pointing toward Molière.

She seemed indifferent to what was happening in the movement of Neo-Latin theater in the university milieu where there were both translations and productions of classical authors. Meanwhile, Marguerite was moving in a quite different direction.

What probably attracted her to this art form in the first place was the same motivation that drew her toward storytelling, a love of seeing people engaged in animated discourse. Her plays were not meant just to be read, but to be performed. And they were.

The French public had always loved the theater. Several professional acting guilds such as the *Clercs de la Basoche* and the *Enfants sans souci* which concentrated on secular plays, and the *Confrérie de la Passion* specializing in religious drama were assured of enthusiastic and supportive audiences even on into the Renaissance.

It was not appropriate, however, for a member of the royal family to work with any of these groups. She may well have seen productions, but the queen's own plays were performed in court for a court audience. Her actors were more likely than not aristocratic ladies like herself. It is indeed quite imaginable that, given her lively and amicable personality, the Queen of Navarre often treaded the boards herself, much no doubt, to the delight and enjoyment of her applauding friends. It is also quite possible that she had hired some professionals, only too happy to accommodate the king's sister.

As for form, it will not be much before the end of the eighteenth century that French playwrights would eventually replace poetry by prose. Although the silly bourgeois, M. Jourdain, in Molière's *Le Bourgeois Gentilhomme*, was amazed to learn that all of his life he had been speaking prose and didn't know it, he might well have made that astounding realization in well-constructed Alexandrian lines.

While preferring eight and ten syllable verse and rhymed couplets or an ABA rhyme scheme, Marguerite quite readily modified her format to suit the specific dramatic need of the moment.

There are no divisions into acts, but rather a sequence of scenes. Her plays offer little or no directions, and we must only imagine that a lot is left to the cleverness and skills of individual performers. As for a stage, in any formal sense of that word, it must also be presumed that these performances took place in private spaces—with a minimum of stage effects.

Finally a word about terminology: the queen seems to have used the labels "farce" and "comédie" rather indiscriminately neither one suggesting our modern idea of these. There is certainly a great deal of humor in her secular pieces, but most of it is didactic and satirical in nature.

Her earliest attempts did not stray from medieval models steeped in Biblical themes. Dating from about 1535, *La nativité, Les trois roys, Les innocents,* and *Le desert* tell in rather dry and uninspired verse the story of Jesus' birth. Only serious students of the French theater of the Middle Ages would want to look at these mystery plays, little more than training ground for the burgeoning artist. Marguerite soon left behind her *Moralities* and *Miracles* and turned to subjects of more contemporary interest.

In a quite different sense, one can say that her first secular piece was indeed something of a miracle. *Le Mallade* strikes one as the creation of an experienced playwright, someone with a long stretch of plays behind her. Some would say she was a natural.

Like all the productions to come, this one consists of short scenes, composed principally in octosyllabic verse. The stage represents two parallel decors, the sick man's bedroom to one side, and the doctor's office to the other. There are only four characters, husband and wife, chambermaid, and doctor. It is, in brief, minimalist and probably quite playable even today.

In an opening scene, we immediately learn of the husband's ailment: *Je sens au cousté grant doulleur* ("I feel great pain on my side"). He expresses his need for a *bon médecin.* The skeptical wife, precursor to the hero in Molière's *Malade Imaginaire*, makes clear her prejudice against the entire medical profession: *Toujours à eulx voulez courir: / Mais leur patte est trop dangereuse* ("You always go running after them / But their paws are too dangerous"). Her own medical advice is much more down to earth, a more naturalistic kind of medication: *Car si seullement voulliez boire/*

Cinq germes d'oeufs tant seullement / Vous verriez bien changer l'histoire ("If you would only drink five young chicks in formation, just that much alone, you would surely see things differently").

In the following scene, we are introduced to the chambermaid, once again a wonderfully smart Molièresque prototype, who becomes the author's spokesperson. Her remedy has less to do with the body and more to do with the soul. When she suggests another kind of healer, he wants to know who it might be. To this she responds: *C'est Dieu, lequel fermement croy / Que tous vos maulx oustera* ("It is God I firmly believe who will take away all your ailments"). But she does not stop her preaching with that fervent declaration of faith. One of the longest speeches in the play follows, all in the religious mode. Her lecture would not appear to have been spoken in vain, for the master replies, *En bonne foy je congnois bien / Que de Dieu vient toute santé* ("In unwavering faith I perfectly recognize that complete health comes from God").

The action then switches to the other side of the stage where the wife is in conversation with the doctor. From the start, in order to make him a mock figure, Marguerite puts pompous and condescending words into the mouth of the doctor: *S'il vous plait me dire la chose / A fin que j'y puisse pourveoir / Ma commère, vouldrois savoir / Quel mal il a* ("Tell me what we are dealing with so that I might give it some reflection. Dear neighbor, I would like to learn the nature of his problem"). Impatient with the doctor's Latin gibberish, she tells him that in her own home style learning, she had just that very morning served him a "drink of pigeon poop."

True scientist that he is, the doctor ignores her and insists on examining his patient: *Le parler icy ne vault guère / Entrons que je touche son poulx* ("Talking is a waste of time / Let me go and check his pulse").

At this juncture, Marguerite supplies one of her rare stage directions: *Icy touche le poulx et le Mallade s'esveille* ("The doctor takes his pulse and awakens the sick man").

Checking his urine and his eyes, the doctor proposes the universal treatment of the day—bloodletting—to which the wife says she has seen many a cure without it. Her impertinent interference with modern science annoys him: *Taisez-vous, folle que vous estes* ("Shut up, crazy woman that you are").

It is then the chambermaid's turn to make light of the doctor's remedies. She sees the problem as moral and not pathological. The sick man's real cause of pain is his wicked ways. He must turn over his life to a more

Christian outlook on things and fight off the *Malin* ("the evil one").

Meanwhile, the doctor asks for his payment. He is not only sure of his intellectual superiority but expects to be paid for it.

When the sick man seems to have recovered, the maid, like a brash Molièresque servant, takes all the credit, arguing that her advanced medicine has more to do with the soul than the body. The arrogant doctor is half convinced . . . *car je croy / Que Dieu fait miracles et signes* ("For I believe that God is capable of miracles and signs"). But not enough to forgo his privileges as a trained scientist. He leaves, lambasting both wife and chambermaid for their ignorance.

The last word is saved for the sick man, for, in a real sense, he is the central figure. Without altogether discounting medical wisdom, he favors the chambermaid's medicine and decides to put his health in the hands of God.

There are no doubt some moments of tiresome preaching here, but considering that this was her first try at a secular setting, Marguerite shows real skill in depicting characters. It is easy to imagine her play winning enthusiastic laughter from an appreciative audience.

There was no inquisition in France. Instead, religious opposition came by way of the conservative Faculty of Theology at the University of Paris. Thanks to these authoritative *Sorbonniquers* figures, by the close of the 1520s, tension was growing measurably worse every year. More and more reformers were being burned at the stake in the infamous Place de Grève. Those with reformist thoughts looked on in fear and horror; many went underground.

In April of 1529, Marguerite learned that one of her favoured protégés, Louis de Berquin, along with all of his heretical books had gone up in flames. It was becoming harder and harder to turn to her brother for help; they were governed by different motivations. As Marguerite worked behind the scene to protect the liberal-minded, her brother, the king, had as his first obligation to safeguard the church and the state.

The friction between the siblings put a great strain on their former affection. The religious conflict was the single most important factor in their growing uneasiness.

It reached a head when, in 1534, some furious and frustrated reformists attacked the church with audacious broadsides, plastering their posters up in major urban centers, even under the very nose of the king. This so-called Placard Affair ought to have silenced the reformist sister, and in one sense it did. She left town. But in another, it did not.

Her next play confronted the changing climate in a piece she called *L'Inquisiteur.* Her attack was subtle, but there could be little doubt that she was sending a message.

Like its predecessor, it is an unbroken sequence of scenes, composed of a variety of rhyming lines, and introducing for the first time the longer and more dramatic decasyllable. A haughty inquisitor, his submissive assistant *(le varlet),* and a group of playing children are the essential characters.

The opening scene consists of a long tirade by the inquisitor who begins his speech with: *Le temps s'en va tousjours empirant* ("The times grow forever worse and worse"). We know we are in for another didactic story, and in order to establish the mood, the playwright is eager to have this character self-importantly identify himself: *Grant temps y a que je suis passé docteur / Dedans Paris par ceulx de la Sorbonne* ("It's been a goodly length of time now that in Paris I was awarded my doctorate from the teachers at the Sorbonne"). To say this is to tell the audience that he is automatically a guardian of the status quo.

In a rare moment, Marguerite gives us an awareness of the action's physical surroundings. The inquisitor wants to stroll to take advantage of the good weather. His servant replies: *Où voulez-vous aller mon maistre, /En ce temps, qui est si diver*("Where, good master, do you want to go in this so unpredictable weather?")

Marguerite thus cleverly sets the stage for the important chance meeting with young children playing outdoors.

The encounter does not start out well. In an imperious voice he says to the children: *Vous feriez myeulx d'estudier.* ("You would do better to study.") He goes on to reprimand: *Voulez-vous donq estre ignorns, /Et perdre ainsi vostre jeunesse* ("Do you wish to remain uneducated /And therefore waste your youth?")

It isn't long before we realize in what direction the dialogue is moving. The inquisitor wants to know who the father is of the boy he criticizes. With a precocious wisdom well beyond his years, the child responds that his father is the one in Heaven. The servant tries to calm the master down as the children then begin to sing a song in praise of love of the divine.

Their song wins over the servant as he cites the Bible: *Mon maistre, dans les vaisseaulx vieulx, / Lon ne mect point les vins nouveaulx* ("Master, one does not put new wine into old vessels"). All of which eventually touches the heart of the inquisitor who asks: *Moy, qui suis vieillard devenu /Puis je renaistre de nouveau* ("I who have become an old man /Can I be born anew?").

Finally persuaded, he says: *Je veulx estre enfant, non plus saige* ("I want to be, not a wise man but a child").

Marguerite, mystic and reformist, preaches that the route to God does not require the preaching of the learned authorities. The meaningful negotiation is between the innocent and pure believer/child and a loving and generous Father. The inquisitor and servant alike adopt this new personal engagement with the Divine, and the play concludes with everyone singing a song of praise.

It all seems harmless enough, but given the growing uneasiness in the country, Marguerite's demeaning of the supercilious inquisitor has to be interpreted as a criticism of the conservative theologians at the Sorbonne with whom she has already had unpleasant dealings.

In 1542 after a silence of four years, during which time the queen was most likely working on her famous collection of short fiction, she returned to the stage once again, and to that other social burning issue of the day, the woman problem, so-called *Querelle des femmes*.

It was a hot topic, but Marguerite could not help but notice that most of the opinions were coming from men. The satirical Rabelais had devoted an entire book of his collection of giant stories to the subject, and several essays by male authors were being circulated about. It was time, she concluded, that women had their say.

Like her contemporary, Rabelais, she sees her new play as a polemic on the question of whether to love or not to love, whether to marry or not to marry. Her *Comédie des quatre femmes* is her theatrical response to these questions and, as was her wont, she envisioned the entire thorny conundrum in dialectical terms, that is, as a debate.

The four main nameless characters consist of two unmarried and two married women who ask: (1) Should one marry, and if so, (2) which partner is most likely to be unfaithful? Final judgment is placed in the hands of a fifth character, *La Vieille,* whose years of accumulated wisdom is supposed to bring reason to the discussion. For a number of scenes, the arguments go back and forth, each woman defending her own position. It is easy to imagine how much Marguerite's exchange amused the court ladies, some of whom surely performed in the play, and all of whom probably discussed the events afterward.

The first young unmarried woman emphatically says: *Quant est de moy, j'ay mise mon estude /D'avoir le corps, et le coeur libre et franc* (As far as I am concerned, I am concentrating on keeping both my heart and my body free and unattached"). Her rival argues rather that there is no happier place than *Au pays d'Amour* ("In love's land")

As for the two married women, one falsely accused of jealousy and the other haunted by it, each stakes her claim.

It is at this juncture that the old lady makes her grand entrance. She begins by offering her credentials—twenty years free, twenty more married, and a final sixty as a widow—accordingly at one hundred, she feels fully qualified to referee.

Does she succeed? Her counsel has more impact on the married women than on the young. The former women hope to conquer their fear and anxieties while the younger remain adamant in their opinions.

In the end, with the sudden appearance of four young gentlemen, the whole thing evolves into a merry dance hinting at the many ballets interlaced into Molière's own comedies, a full century later.

As a theatrical experience, the play leaves much to be desired. The long speeches may have amused the contemporary audience, many of whom knew each other. By today's standards, it could only have historical value for feminists.

None of Marguerite's plays has engendered more consternation and confusion among interpreters than *Trop, Prou, Peu, Moins*. There is little agreement among critics about its true meaning. And that may be because Marguerite may not have taken the work very seriously herself. It's labelled a *farce*.

In his opening remarks, *Trop* (too much) reveals his essential pomposity when he says: *Ma Seigneurie, et mon office / Mon estat, / et mon exercise / Est plus grand, que toute la Terre* ("My possessions and my office / My estate and my profession are more significant than the whole world"). His companion *Prou* (much) follows suit in announcing in the same self-important voice: *Je ne veux point avoir de maistre / Ne servir à nul, fors à moy* ("I do not want to have a master / Nor to serve anyone but myself").

We learn that Trop and Prou are related: *Ne mecongnoisez-vous, mon Fils / Je suis Trop vostre pere grand* ("Have you forgotten me, my son / I am Trop, your grandfather").

They are not only related but also bound by distinguishing psychological and physical traits. When Trop brags of never tiring of wealth, his son echoes his sentiments: *J'ay tousjours peur de n'avoir rien* ("I am forever scared of having nothing"). Upon discovering that they also share having ears, they are ashamed and wish to do what they can to hide this *meschef* ("handicap").

In like manner, the second pair, Peu and Moins, is similarly twinned in characteristic attributes. They each acknowledge their insignificance. Moins humbly remarks: *Je me nomme le povre Moins / Le moindre de tous les humains* ("I am called Less / the least among humans"). Whereas the earlier couple hide their disgraceful physical link, their ears, the other pair takes pride in their horns which protect them against all difficulties.

At the point where the four eventually meet up, there is an immediate philosophical clash. The second pair takes satisfaction in announcing that they are always happy, that indeed their greatest weapon is joy and laughter. Meanwhile, Prou confesses: *Jamais au coeur nous n'avons joye* ("We never have joy in our hearts"). If for the one duo everything is good and beautiful, for the other all is evil and ugly. Thus, like the innocent children in *L'Inquisiteur,* the triumphant voices here are those of Peu and Moins who sponsor laughter and joy.

Putting aside all other potential theological or political implications, the essential message may not go beyond that.

Goodness knows that Marguerite in her lifetime had had her share of grieving for family members: her mother Louise, her sister-in-law the queen, her aunt Philiberte, and her favourite young niece Charlotte. But nothing, absolutely nothing, could compare with the death of the brother to whom she was so intimately attached since childhood. When she heard the news of his sickness in the spring of 1547, Marguerite, as we remember, immediately set out to be by his bedside. She never got to her destination. Her grieving gave birth to her next play.

Comédie sur le trespass du roy is written in the form of a pastoral dialogue with all the characters bearing Latin names. The playwright assigns the opening lines to herself, in the guise of the Amarissime. The distraught shepherdess, in stately and elegiac decasyllables, bemoans the death of the great god of the wild: *Mais est-il vray, est-ce chose assurée / Que Pan nous est osté de ces bas lieux* ("Is it true, is it confirmed / that Pan has been removed from these lowly parts?"). For more than fifty lines, she decries the overwhelming significance of the terrible loss, ending in a dirgelike melody which, in a rare stage direction, Marguerite informs us is to be sung on the well-known tune, *Jouyssance vous donneray.*

She intermittently continues to sing as Securus expresses his own intense pain by asking her to stop mournful singing: *Cesse ce chant et ces pleurs lamentables / Qui n'est à corps ny esprit profitable* ("Stop this singing and these miserable tears which are good for neither body nor soul").

After another shepherd, Agapy, gives vent to his unhappiness, Securus reminds them all of their common fate: *Sçais-tu bien que l'homme est né Pour tout ou tard ung jour mourir* ("Do you not realize that sooner or later we are all one day to die?") This is a remark which the stoic Christian Marguerite puts into her companion's mouth and thus leads to the introduction of the last member of this group of grievers, Paraclesis.

As messenger from on high, he completes Securus's recent plea for resignation by telling them that their god, Pan, who is now out of danger and pain, *ne veult point que sa gloire l'on pleure* ("does not wish one to weep for his glory"). Paraclesis has the final word when he declares: *Or, chantons donc, tout d'un accord/Puisque Pan est vivant, non mort* ("Let us thus join in song since Pan is not dead but alive"). The song in question is a Latin citation from the Gospel according to John, urging one to reach out for the hand of a loving God.

Thus concludes Marguerite's deeply felt if rather stylized homage to a much loved and admired dead brother. One wonders if the subject lent itself to this art form. Her play might have been far more successful in the form of a panegyric poem which it in fact strives to become.

Still grieving and feeling the stress and strain of old age, Marguerite progressively chose to eschew the din and clatter of court life. In 1547, surrounded by a few friends and limited staff, she took up residence in the quiet and off-the-beaten-track south western town of Mont-de-Marsan. If her body was failing the queen, her mind certainly was not. In her penultimate play, *Comédie de Mont-de-Marsan*, she explores the philosophical question of how best to live one's life now that she is approaching the end of her own. She frames the issue in the form of a debate among four women; there are no men in this discussion!

Each character gets a turn at defining her raison d'être. The first to expound her views is *La Mondaine* ("The Worldly One") who says*: Jayme mon corps, demandez moy pourquoy: /Parce que beau and plasiant je le voy* ("I love my body, ask me why: because I find it beautiful and attractive"). She has no interest in this thing called the soul which she can't even see.

Next in line is *La Supersticieuse* ("The Superstitious One"), who is planning a pilgrimage to the tomb site of Sainte Brigette, where she will pray for the salvation of her soul. *La Sage* ("The Wise One"), on the other hand, makes much of the happy fact that God has given man a special gift, his intelligence, to set him apart from the rest of the animal kingdom.

The ensuing dialogue is devoted to a lively exchange between the worldly and religious women, each trying to convince the other of the justice of her beliefs. While the one takes pleasure in the joys of nature: *Il est jour, dict alouette / Surtout, alons jouer sur l'herbette* ("It is daybreak, said the lark / let us above all go and dance in the grass"), the other, more somber and serious, sings praises to the Virgin Mary.

Meanwhile, *La Sage* thanks God for giving humans the power to reason and think.

What follows then is a discussion on the essential nature of man; is it more physical or more spiritual? To which the *La Sage* appropriately says: *Mais, l'ame au corps joincte et unie / C'est l'homme . . .* ("But body joined and united with soul, that is man . . ."). And so it goes until the final personage comes forward, a singing shepherdess who seems to have very little time for or interest in these solemn ruminations. The more the other three try to engage with her, the more she eludes them in songs that make no real sense. In short, it is once again Marguerite's marked preference for the simple and the unassuming over the deep and serious-minded.

There is an obvious irony in the queen's position, one to which she returns regularly. For at the same time that she argues for the childlike unexamined life, she examines her own incessantly.

Certainly, most of this theater today would be quite unplayable. And yet they tell us much about the philosophical issues that plagued Marguerite. They are important to anyone interested in having a better grasp of who she was and what she thought. What is more, at her most inspired, the Queen of Navarre is not at all lacking in persuasive character analysis and even, on occasion, a good laugh.

POETRY

No one would think to nominate Marguerite for a prominent place in the pantheon of French poets alongside such greats as Villon, Hugo, or Rimbaud. But the queen wrote lots of altogether competent poetry in her lifetime, ranging from the clever and entertaining to the thoughtful and serious. They pretty well divide up into two general categories: religious and secular.

RELIGIOUS

When Marguerite first thought to put her ideas down on paper, it often came out in the form of a rhymed dialogue. She was, after all, an avid conversationalist who loved talking and loved listening to other's talk. As for opting for verse over prose, until more recent times, if anyone had anything important to say, it was said in verse. Prose does not replace verse until the eighteenth century.

It was heartache and personal anguish which led Marguerite to take pen in hand. In October of 1524, Charlotte, a favourite niece and second daughter to the king, died of rubella. Her apprehensive and prayerful aunt had sat for nearly a month by Charlotte's bedside until the poor child breathed her last; she was not yet nine years of age. Although Marguerite had experienced death in the family before, the disappearance of this young niece left her perplexed and questioning. It was in that depressed state of mind, *pis que morte* ("worse than dead"), that she composed *Le Dialogue en forme de vision nocturne* ("Dialogue in the Form of a Nocturnal Vision").

The poet begins: *L'ennuy trop grief de la dure nouvelle / . . . Me fut si grant, que je croys qu'oncques femme / Telle douleur ne pourroit soutenir* ("So gravely troubled was I by this cruel news / . . . that I think no woman / ever had to bear such sorrow"). And then for over a thousand lines in the difficult Italian *terza rima* (rhymed triplets) format, she engaged in a dense theological discussion in which it is the resurrected child who must comfort the grieving aunt. It is throughout a lesson in Christian forbearance that the prescient and precocious Charlotte preaches, suggesting that for a true Christian, death is a beginning and not an end. The inconsolable aunt should rejoice that her niece has found happiness far from the distress and suffering of this fractured mortal existence.

The poem must have been written immediately after the event, but Marguerite did not get around to having it published much before 1533.

Is it also possible that Marguerite hesitated because she did not yet feel sure about its literary worth? We know that, years later, when she was anthologizing her works, she left it out of the collection.

One day, an English tutor gave her twelve-year-old pupil a French text to translate—no extraordinary event except that the girl was the future Queen Elizabeth of

England; the author Marguerite de Navarre and the text *Le Miroir de l'âme pécheresse* ("Mirror of a Sinful Soul"). It was probably her most important and popular religious poem.

This prolix verse confession, running over 1400 decasyllabic couplets, is a model of sixteenth century evangelistic piety. One of the chief characteristics of this kind of religious poetry is the sinner's strong sense of guilt, promptly established when the narrator speaks of her countless sins: . . . *en si grand nombre / qu'infinitude rend si obscure l'ombre / Que les compter ne les bien veoir je ne puys* ("in such great numbers that the infinite quantity keeps me from either counting or taking them all in"). This self-denigrating theme fills the pages of the poem: *Et qu'humblement en pleurant je confesse / Que quant à moy, je suis trop moins que rien* ("And that all in tears, I humbly confess / And as for me, I amount to much less than nothing"). She writes: *Helas! Je voy de mes maulx la laydeur* ("Alas, I see the ugliness of my flaws"). With exaggeration, she bemoans that she is little better than a worm.

We find this kind of self-deprecation altogether hostile to our own taste in poetry, but it had a real audience in sixteenth-century France, particularly in reformist circles. Thus in a proto-protestant idiom, Marguerite prays for her soul, finding comfort in a deity who is related to her, sometimes as sister, sometimes as brother, and sometimes even as spouse: *Couvrant à tous ma faulte et delict / Me redonnant part de vostre lict* ("You covered up my shortcomings and flaws from everyone, / Sharing your bed with me").

This kind of familial intimacy exemplifies the language of the mystic, and Marguerite proves herself efficient in that style. In fact, some modern-day evangelists would appreciate the way she speaks of her Lord: *Mort est Jesus, en qui tous mortz nous sommes, /*

Et en sa mort faict vivre tous ses hommes ("Jesus died, in whose death we are all participants and whose death gave life to all"). They would also take pleasure in her extensive knowledge of the scriptures.

Today's evangelistic Protestant would surely take note of Marguerite's fervent celebration of the *bienheureux* ("Blessed") Saint Paul whom she addresses at the close of the poem. She begs him to intercede on her behalf and to correct her *ignorance et faulte* ("ignorance and flaws).

What in the end prompts this kind of self-critical analysis so foreign to most religious readers of our own time? Only a different spiritual context can explain the phenomenon. Marguerite knows she has a potential readership. On the one hand, she wishes to be useful to others who might find her confessional style instructive. But she is also quite selfishly motivated. This is a cathartic exercise common to the mystical mind. She fully realizes that a just and generous God will overlook her flaws and grant, in a true reformist way of reasoning, undeserved grace, given without conditions and restrictions. Marguerite places wholehearted hope over despair, faith over works to God: *Ne puis faillir à rendre la louenge / De tant de biens qu'avoir que je ne merite / Que lui plasit faire de moys sa Marguerite . . . Amen* ("I must not fail to sing praises / For all the blessings I have and do not deserve / [Of him who] it was pleasing to bestow on me, Marguerite . . . Amen").

Le Miroir had no less than eleven editions published in Marguerite's own lifetime, a clear indication that she judged correctly an avid and ready readership for this kind of confessional soul-baring style of writing. It may seem strangely overstated and attention grabbing to our modern ears; it did not to those who shared her theological point of view.

In the minds of many, Marguerite's *Les Prisons* is her theological magnum opus. It was a lifetime project she had begun sometime in the 1530s but a work in progress until before her death. In a sprawling six thousand rhymed decasyllabic lines, an unnamed narrator, merely identified as *L'Amy*, reviews his perilous march toward divine knowledge. He is describing this spiritual journey to an anonymous *LAmye*, assumed to have at one time been his mistress.

In a sense therefore, the entire text is answering one of Marguerite's favored philosophical questions: To what do we commit our lives?

In the first section he speaks of his burdensome love of love. He describes how he was for a long while a besotted fool, a veritable "prisoner" to this woman whose very voice was an enchantment to him. He argues that: . . . *estre grand et puissant terrien /*

Sans estre aymé et aymer, ce n'est rien ("greatness and power in this world / without being loved or loving, are nothing"). But when he learns of her infidelity, he understands that this kind of search for happiness leads to disappointment and disillusionment: *Or adieu donc, ma prison et mon tour / où je ne veux jamais faire retour / Adieu l'abisme où j'estoys englouty / Adieu le feu où souvent fust rosty / Adieu la glace où mainte nuits tremblay* ("Farwell then to my prison and to my tour / To which I never want to return / Farewell to the abyss where I was engulfed / Farewell to the fire in which I often was scalded / Farwell to the ice where many a night I shivered"). Students of the love poetry of the Renaissance will recognize the popular images from which Marguerite borrows.

Freed from his first prison, *L'Amy* sets out on another search for fulfillment, this time the search for the dubious rewards of the material world.

In an unusual awareness of natural phenomena in Marguerite's writings, the narrator is awed by the beauty he sees around him: trees, fields, bodies of water. He then travels to great cities, and visits important courts where he is dazzled by the wealth and by the handsome and elegant people in them.

But just as he is about to be won over by material splendour and luxury, he meets an old man who warns him against the potential entrapment of such deceiving temptations. The world of material happiness is not as wonderful as he might think. It is, on the contrary, a complete fraud. From one moment to the next, the rich and the powerful must remain alert because everything can suddenly be taken away from them. For this too is delight in appearance only, a mere illusion. Certainly, the queen was thoroughly familiar with this sort of extravagant affluence; she lived in the midst of it. But as a committed Christian, she was not unaware of its fleeting gratification.

And so, once again frustrated, *L'Amy* resumes his pursuit of happiness.

Book III, twice as long as I and II put together, is by far the most complex and also the least structurally coherent, for Marguerite allows herself many digressions of personal remembrances.

Having learned a thing or two about the world's many ruses and shams, he begins by telling *L'Amy* that perhaps the most treacherous of all deceits are those of the intellect. Learning also can be a prison, for it gives one a false sense of power and sway. This is an opportunity for Marguerite to take a swipe at theological books. Of course, she is thinking specifically of those put out by the conservative press at the Sorbonne.

On the other hand, can this be the same Marguerite who had all of her life thirsted after knowledge? Is the Queen of Navarre questioning her own highly intellectual ambitions so much a part of who she had always been?

Through the voice of *L'Amy*, she reminds her readers that all knowledge, all wisdom, all eloquence comes from the Almighty. No thinker achieves anything *Si la vertu de Dieu ne luy permet* ("If God's power does not allow it"). And that power is best discovered in Holy Script. And once we have that special knowledge, we are able to see it elsewhere. In short, we must not depend upon our *cuydance* ("presumption"). The mental strength we require is that which is provided by the divine. It is that power which defies all fears, up to and including the fear of death.

This observation leads Marguerite to remember the important fallen dead in her own life: her first husband Charles and his mother Claude de Lorraine, her own mother, and brother. As the long poem thus comes to its close, the voice of the fictional narrator gives way to that of the author's. Marguerite ends *Les Prisons* with a final song of praise to God, all expressed in her own personal name.

This may indeed be deemed as Marguerite's most profound spiritual autobiography and a source for a better understanding of how she interprets the universal human search for fulfillment. But it does raise one basic question that has not escaped its critics: Why she opted to put it all in the voice of a fictional character, not only fictional, but male? However one finally resolves that issue, this is a monumental work of analysis, both philosophical and psychological and convincing proof of the author's ability to probe a complicated question, and all in verse.

SECULAR

Not the entire Queen of Navarre's intellectual querying is religious. Some questions that excite her imagination are altogether secular in nature. And what is more secular than a letter?

There is today—no doubt because these were members of royalty—a huge collection of letters written by Marguerite and her relations, all very valuable to scholars, not only wanting to learn something about the family itself, but also about what was happening in the world surrounding them. The clever and ingenious trio did not, however, settle for ordinary everyday prose. Many of their epistles were composed in verse, and

Marguerite may well have been the most adept at this kind of writing. Here are just a few examples which allow us to understand the scope and cleverness of her verse epistles.

The first example dates from 1530 and is addressed to her mother, Louise de Savoy, who had gone down to Bordeaux to meet her grandchildren, hostages being released from the Spanish court after the disastrous French defeat at the battle of Pavia. Marguerite bemoans the fact that her pregnancy has kept her from joining her mother on this happy occasion but rejoices at the thought of a family reunited. Remembering who she is, she sees the good news as: *Le bien, et l'heur, et delice de France* ("The wealth, the joy, and the delight of France"). This is not, after all, only an aunt, a daughter, and a sister speaking, but a royal princess. The style is amazingly spontaneous and evidence of Marguerite's quick wit.

The birth in 1544 of a royal grandchild inspires another verse letter, this one to her brother, but not any brother, but a brother who happens to be the King of France. While Marguerite emphasizes the importance of the event from its political point of view, she is not beyond being a bit glib and even flippant. Who can doubt his legitimacy, she asks? One need only look at his *bien grand nés* ("very generous nose"), the unmistakable trademark not only of Valois authenticity but the sign, she seems to imply, of male prowess.

Nevertheless, she speaks out of genuine pride and concludes her congratulatory poem with the best wishes of a delighted great aunt: *Rien plus ça bas ne veux, ne n'ay envie / Fors de sa bonne, heureuse and longue vie* ("I desire and long for nothing more in this world / Except for his good, happy, and long life"). We would have sent a store-bought card.

The next verse letter has its recipient as none other than Henri d'Albret, Marguerite's second husband and father of their child, Jeanne. Composed in 1547, it is a precious document, a very rare intimate message from Marguerite to her husband who has fallen ill and from whom she regrets being absent: *O quel ennuy d'estre de vous bannie / Et vous lasser en telle compagnie / D'extreme mal et de douleur cruelle* ("O what anguish to be far from you / And to leave you in the bad company / Of stinging pain and cruel agony"). Marguerite married a man with whom she truly fell in love and whom she continued to love to the very end.

This is a unique piece since there is not much else written to connect this famous couple and to underscore Marguerite's affections for this spouse of over twenty years.

The letter has an incidental value for students of French Renaissance literature. When she wanted to express her impatience in hearing good news about her husband's improved health, she likened her anxiety to an episode in Rabelais's *Pantagruel.* Not that we needed to be reminded, but it is evidence of Marguerite's keen awareness of the literature of her day.

The final verse letter here is no doubt the most startling in tone and message. It could have been written in the middle of the Romantic era, but was in fact composed in 1549, the very last year of Marguerite's life and sent to her daughter Jeanne, newly wedded to Antoine de Bourbon. It is the love song of a grieving mother who misses a daughter with whom she can never again have quite the same relationship.

It begins thus, love comes to her in the middle of the night: *Amour me vient tout soudain esveiller / Disant:'Escriptz et prens la plume en main* ("Love came to me suddenly and woke me up / Saying: 'Take up your pen and write'"). She must not keep her daughter, she is told, waiting any longer. Fully acknowledging her aging body and tired mind, Marguerite wants her peace of mind: *J'ay tant escript* ("I have written so much") and she has. We immediately feel in those few short painful words the tension between a sentimental mother and a tired old lady.

Nevertheless, a mother's emotions prevail. The weary queen obediently takes up her pen and looks for a quiet spot in her garden to write. Then, like some Romantic poet of the nineteenth century, Marguerite describes the wonderful music all around her, a veritable symphony of sounds created by *Les petites fontaines* ("small fountains") and *la voix de la riviere* ("the voice of the river"). And what does the music say? *Helas! Helas! Or l'avons nous perdue? / Las! dessus nous ne tourne plus sa vue* ("Alas! Alas! Have we lost her? / Alas, she no longer looks our way").

Giving in to her maternal instincts, the grieving mother begs God to return to this desolate place: *Celle que tant ciel et terre regrette / Et que revoir incessamment souhaitte* ("She whom heaven and earth lament / The one they yearn to see once more"). This is a rare moment when Marguerite is neither queen nor princess; she is just another sad and lonely mother.

In those closing years, Marguerite's mind continued to be vigorously agile and quite up to the kind of prolix verse writing she had always been capable of. In 1541, she composed not one but two hefty poems, both dealing with gender relations. The poetic structure of each, however, differs radically as we shall see. They are each one proof of exceptional intelligence, if not great poetry.

La Coche ("The Coach") borrows its idea from an old medieval genre, in which several opposing speakers express views on a given theme, to be adjudicated in the end to determine which debater has triumphed. Marguerite uses the formula but makes significant changes.

If the subject—which of three women has suffered the most in her love life—does not surprise us, the conclusion and the way the poet goes about telling her story diverge significantly from the conventional structure. Marguerite creates a strikingly original hybrid of narrative and theater.

Prior to each scene, an anonymous storyteller/playwright, who is not Marguerite, offers stage directions, all composed in prose. These directions announce a series of "stories" which are in fact more like scenes in a play. In the first of these directorial prose passages, we are told, for example, that we are in a quiet meadow: *Au bout duquel est une femme comme la Royne de Navarre, cheminant par une petite sente* ("at the end of which there is a woman resembling the Queen of Navarre proceeding along a small path"). In a verse monologue, this woman, who seems to be Marguerite, complains of her loss of love and even the loss of that once important pleasure which came from writing. But at present, she enjoys the loveliness of her surroundings where the very greenery seems to be *plein d'esperance* ("full of hope"). She engages in a friendly conversation with a peasant when, suddenly, out of the woods appear three women, all dressed in black. They approach and tell her she would do better to talk to them than with this *fascheux paisant* ("uninspired peasant").

It turns out they are not just any three ladies, but friends of hers and all very depressed and all keen on telling their stories. We learn from these tales of woe that two are involved with the same man who has abandoned one to take up with the other. In the meantime, the third woman scorns their sorrows and the whole business of love and is herself quite prepared to give up her own *serviteur* ("courtly lover") in order to join forces with her friends. In short, she recommends the revolutionary idea of opting for female bonding over unhappy and unsatisfying relations with men: *Que perdez-vous? Ung maulvais et ung fainct* ("What do you give up? A bad and a false [lover]").

We recall that this is meant to be a contest to ascertain who of the three is the saddest. Respecting the formula of the debate genre, they must find a just and reliable arbiter. The first lady suggests the king himself, Marguerite's brother Francis I providing a perfect opportunity to sing his countless virtues.

Marguerite immediately balks at this outrageous suggestion. In a kind of false modesty, she dares not put her meagre scribbling before the eyes of such a *parfaict esprit* ("perfect mind"). A second lady puts forward Marguerite herself as judge which prompts a most curious and very self-revealing response from the narrator: *Mes cinquante ans, ma vertue affoyblie / le temps passé commandent que j'oublye / Pour mieulx penser à la prochaine mort* ("My fifty years, my failing health / demand that I forget the past / In order to think better about my approaching death").

This highly personal comment seems to come out of nowhere, but the ladies acquiesce and try to conjure up the name of another dependable adjudicator. They finally settle on the person of the Duchess d'Etampes, the king's very mistress and the one for whom this entire poem was being written. And so we easily grasp the nature of this flattering decision. It is bound to be a good one, pleasing to king, mistress, and sister.

This very long and rather mind-numbing poem is no easy text for the modern reader to appreciate, but most feminists would have to agree an important moment in the slow march toward gender equality.

La Fable du faux cuyder ("The Fable About False Pride"), written in the same year as the preceding poem, is, by comparison, a far lighter and jauntier piece. Its ten syllable couplets dance more effortlessly across the page, and it is easy to imagine Marguerite not only enjoying the writing of her poem but her amusement in reading it to a consenting like-minded audience of lady friends.

It was, in any event, composed for her namesake niece who was getting married and is thus something of a cautionary tale placed in a classical frame. The moral is laid out from the very start: *Et n'ont Cuyder, Desir, ny Esperance, / Nul fondement, qu'aveuglée Ignorance* ("Pride, Desire, and Hope have no other origin than blind Ignorance"). With that opening comment, many allegorical figures come alive in a verse narrative that does not seem either heavy-handed or tiresome.

The poet situates the scene in a pastoral setting where a cluster of Satyrs espy the goddess Diana's virgins taking in the beautiful weather. Lust fills the hearts of the sex-hungry Satyrs as they watch the lovely creatures sun-bathing within arm's reach. Ready to pounce, they are however reproached for their foolish impetuosity by an older and wiser member of the assemblage who suggests a more cautious strategy. He recommends easygoing seduction instead of an unwise assault. Why not charm with delightful music and dancing?

Diana, meanwhile, ever the protective mother, suspects the danger and encourages her maidens to take advantage of the pleasant setting and indulge in a little outdoor siesta. And so they obediently comply, except for five overly inquisitive maidens.

Approchons-nous, d'avoir mal nous n'avons garde ("Let's get closer, there is nothing to fear"), one proposes. Their curiosity inspires the licentious Satyrs to break into a *son plus plaisant et hautain* ("more pleasing and lively tune"), until these stimulated and eager musicians, no longer able to contain their passion, drop their instruments and prepare for the attack. Diana, ever alert, sees what is happening and swiftly comes to the rescue of her insubordinate and naughty charges.

Then follow two long tirades, a pleading for mercy on the one side and then the predictable reprimand of a loving but angry goddess. Anger, however, is mediated by pity and instead of a harsher punishment, Diana morphs the wayward maidens into weeping willow tress.

She then turns her ire upon the wicked Satyrs who are forced to confess that they were motivated by *fureur sans amour* ("loveless lust").

Marguerite's lesson is that such Satyrs are present everywhere and that the young innocents of this world must be forever on their guard. While it does at first seem like a strange gift to a happy bride just before her marriage, it nevertheless reminds us that the gift giver has herself experienced terrible male deceit and trickery. She is giving her niece the benefit of her own sad experiences. This is the loving warning of an aunt who speaks out of affection and common sense.

In the minds of many, Marguerite reaches the apogee of her poetic skills when inspired by the death of a younger sibling whom she has spent her entire life admiring and looking up to.

Upon hearing of her brother's grave illness, in spite of her own weakened condition, she immediately sets out to be by his bedside. She never makes it.

Tired, she is forced to take refuge at the monastery in the tiny town of Tusson. It is here that the devastating news comes to her. For days, the bereft older sister desperately tries to come to terms with the illogic of the death of a younger sibling. At first, she can do little more than wander about aimlessly, brooding and grieving. Eventually, the unhappy queen is only able to find some relief in "sweet writing," giving birth to an outpouring of deep emotions, not to be matched anywhere else in her poetry.

How can this be, this person who was so much a part of her flesh and blood?: *Je crie par bois at par plains, / Au ciel et terre me complains / A rien fors à mon dueil ne pense* ("Through wood and plain I grieve

/ To heaven and earth I cry out / I think of naught but my sorrow").

Death alone can bring solace to her tormented and aching heart: *O mort, que le Frère as domté / Vien donc par ta grande bonté / Transpercer la Soeur de ta lance* ("O death who has undone the Brother / In your great kindness come / Pierce the Sister with your lance").

But years of sorrow and grief had taught Marguerite that her greatest solace invariably came to her in the comforting experience of writing. And write she did, leaving an amazing legacy only now coming to the attention of the modern reader.

Would the Queen of Navarre have been ready to acknowledge that it would be neither her theatre nor her poetry but her only prose work of consequence that would eventually bring her the posthumous fame she deserved?

THE HEPTAMERON

There was neither radio nor television in those bygone days. People had to amuse themselves in other ways, often in storytelling. Eventually, many of these yarns and legends got written down and by Marguerite's time, there was already a long tradition of published story collections in Italy and France. The queen was conversant in both languages and had read and enjoyed many of these compilations in the original when she decided to create her own French *Decameron*. It was meant to be the third volume of her collected works but death intervened, and Marguerite never progressed beyond novella #72.

Which is why one of her earliest editors entitled her uncompleted manuscript as a *Heptameron,* in other words "seventy" not "one hundred" tales as planned.

Unfortunately, that original manuscript, which presumably went to her daughter, Jeanne, has never been located. As a result, editors over the years have had to rely on a dozen or so subsequent copies—all in various states of completion and accuracy—in order to try to reconstruct what might have been in Marguerite's lost original.

We do know, because she clearly says so in her prologue, that she was imitating a Boccaccio frame device: a narrative pretext to bring ten storytellers together—in his case, the plague, in Marguerite's, a flood high in the Pyrenees Mountains. But there may be as many differences as there are similarities between these two texts.

****

THE STORIES

There is little doubt that she aimed to be entertaining. Anyone who has dipped into Marguerite's anthology has to acknowledge that the Queen of Navarre is a great storyteller. She undoubtedly had had lots of practice among friends with whom she exchanged tales long before ever putting anything down on paper. What kinds of stories are these?

One discovers, in and among the more obvious tales of naughty people doing naughty things, a nucleus of longer courtly romances from an older tradition, far less scabrous and composed in a different tone of voice. Most significantly, they are all attributed to the character called Parlamente, assumed by most scholars to be Marguerite herself.

Instead of the more anecdotal kind of narrative about lustful characters, many of them priests and monks, these distinctly different and longer tales portray men and women engaged in a kind of idealized love or *parfaicte amityé*. In short, they represent a courtly tradition, very much in favor when Marguerite first started collecting her stories. The heroines are invariably highborn ladies and their gentleman lovers, devoted and heroic *serviteurs*: novellas 10, 13, 21, 40, 42, 57, 64, 70.

But tastes were changing rapidly, and Marguerite, astute enough to recognize in what direction the narrative wind was blowing, was quick to switch to a different more down-to-earth style that was coming into fashion.

Leaving behind these courtly tales, she readily adjusts to the new interest in quick, often funny, stories of lovemaking and deceit, stories that would be readily recognizable to her readership. She even insists that her tales, in comparison with those of other writers, would be exclusively "true."

Storytellers must, in a word, speak as if they were reporting news (*nouvelles*). Ever conscious of this restriction, Marguerite's narrators are eager to announce that what they are telling is the truth. Simontaut, for example, starts out by telling his listeners: *et si diray rien que pure verité* ("And so I shall say nothing but the pure truth"). Oisille ends her first tale by assuring everyone that this was *une histoire veritable* ("a true story"). Sometimes, as in novella 15, in order to protect the identity of its well-known hero, the narrator says: *y avoit ung gentil homme, duquel je congnois si bien le nom que je ne le veulx poinct nommer* ("there was a gentleman whose name I know so well that I do not wish to name him").

Is that all that she means by "true?" Are we talking about our modern concept of realism?

Probably not. The modern use of that term usually implies physical detail. There is little or none of that here. When the author wants to situate a text, it is no more than a fleeting opening sentence like: *En la ville de Pampelune, y avoit une dame estimée, belle et vertueuse, et la plus chaste et devote qui fust au pays* ("In the city of Pamplune, there was a lady, highly esteemed, beautiful and virtuous, and the most chaste to be found in all that country")—novella 35.

Description of the material world seems quite beside the point to Marguerite. She tells tales to amuse (novellas 34, 36, 69, 39). She is quite capable of relating a hilarious scatological story that seems more appropriate to preadolescent humor (novella 11). She may even have been the creator of the first ghost story (39), but the larger percentage of stories deal with sexual behaviour where what happens is far more important than how the characters appear when they are performing. Her readers want to know what her actors do rather than how they look.

Although one can point to love stories as examples of model conduct (novellas 9–10, 16, 18–20, 24, 26, 32, 35, 37, 38, 57, 61), more than anything else, her tales speak of sexual mischief, especially those involving Franciscan monks (novellas 3–4, 12, 25, 27, 30, 45, 53, 62, 71). That surely is one kind of realism.

Perhaps her realism is of the social history variety. Marguerite does in fact give us a fairly good picture of what the societal structures of French sixteenth century were like. The bulk of her tales may be set in her own class (novellas 1, 5, 22, 29, 31–34, 40, 42, 46, 48, 57,

72); that after all is what she knew best. But she does not ignore either the rising bourgeoisie (novellas 7, 13, 36, 38, 45, 54, 62, 71) or even, on at least one occasion, the peasant class (novella 2).

But her concept of telling the truth may in fact mean something else entirely. It may have much more to do with, not the stories, but the storytellers.

THE STORYTELLERS

The lively discussions that follow each story reveal much about the dynamics of the people who are narrating so much so that it has been very tempting to scholars to construct a kind of *roman à clef.* But even if there is no reason to assign historical names to all the ten *devisants,* it is a credit to their inventor's psychological skills that critics want to do so. What do we learn about Marguerite's gabby narrators?

Oisille is the *grande dame* of the group. She is indeed "grande," we are told in the prologue, heavyset, and prone to stumbling. But she does not stumble intellectually. It may well be that she not only often expresses the most conservative religious views in the discussions but it is also she who every morning reads and comments on some Biblical passage. That is something only someone with decidedly reformist leanings would do. Moreover, when it comes to moral conduct, she expects as much from women as she does from men. As for historical antecedents, she is likely a combination of Marguerite's mother, Louise de Savoie, and perhaps Marguerite herself.

Nearly everyone agrees that there is much of the author in the person of Parlamente. We are told in the prologue that she is married to the character, Hircan, the excuse for many funny even erotic exchanges between the two of them.

Like her creator, she is an important spokesperson for the Neoplatonic concept of love: *Encores ay-je une opinion que jamais homme n'aymera parfaictement*

Dieu, qu'il n'ait parfaictement aymé quelque creature en ce monde ("I am of the opinion that one will never love God perfectly until one has first perfectly loved some human being of this world").

As for Hircan, he is as non-Platonic as Parlamente is Platonic. The world, especially the sexual privileges of the world, belongs to men. In most discussions, you can expect him to take a totally unromantic, unsentimental view of things, even urging the hero in his abuse of some poor ladylove. If Parlamente is based on Marguerite, it seems most logical that Hircan is her second husband, Henri de Navarre.

From this point on, historical identifications become more and more speculative and uncertain. The character named Longarine is referred to as *la vefe Longarine* ("the widow Longarine"). We learn in the prologue that her husband has been killed. She is described as a generally sensitive and compassionate person. A strong believer in the need for human love, she also understands that it can sometimes lead one astray.

Dagoucin is the most perfect gentleman among all the male storytellers, mild-mannered and soft-spoken. And yet in the prologue, he heroically comes to the defense of the women when they are attacked by brigands. He is not married, one can deduce, but easily charmed by the ladies in the group, notably Parlamente, whose Neoplatonic views he clearly shares. Of the five gentlemen, he is the most outspoken advocate of gender equality.

Saffredent can also be seen as a *serviteur* of Parlamente, yet does not hesitate to support unfaithfulness and to assume that the male animal is a superior being. He readily cites literary sources when he defends a point of view, so one can assume that he is well-educated.

Ennasuite is the most jolly and cheerful among the five women, the first to laugh, with a marked preference for telling stories that amuse. Although married, she has no illusions about men and their search for sexual gratification and totally cynical about the authority of clerics.

Nomerfide—probably the youngest of the women in the group—like Ennasuite, generally opts for stories that inspire laughter. Also like her, she has very little use for men of the cloth. When it comes to love, young and hopeful, she is hopeful but nevertheless thinks it difficult to find Mr. Perfect.

Hircan refers to Geburon as *le plus saige d'entre nous* ("the wisest among us") which does not prevent him from being rather pessimistic about human nature. He even goes so far as to warn women about the evil intentions of his own sex. Like everyone else, he is anticlerical and tells tales to corroborate his negative attitude.

Simontaut is yet another devoted admirer of Parlamente. But when she criticizes his unfaithfulness as a husband, he is quick to tell her that she is quite out of line in commenting on his behaviour. Nevertheless, he shares the widespread cynicism among the storytellers about humans. He seems the most candid about his assumption that men and women have quite different sexual needs and that, by and large, women are the lesser creatures.

****

In brief, because of these sparkling and energetic discussions, we have a real sense of these people. They are far from the stick figures as in Boccaccio's collection. They are convincingly real or "true."

Marguerite tells us in the prologue that she wants to avoid any sort of self-consciously rhetorical tricks. This narrative imperative will apply as much to the way the stories are told as to the storytellers themselves in the discussions that follow. There is a natural ease and unaffected manner among them that persuade us, even if no historical names can be attached to all of them, that Marguerite has observed well the world around her.

The most absorbing example of this is the relationship between the author herself, Parlamente, and her husband, Hircan. And while it is perilous to turn fiction into biography, there is much that is revealed in the rapport of this married couple that defines not just two impassioned people but members of an entire society.

Already in the prologue, we learn something about this sixteenth-century relationship. In spite of the place generally granted to Marguerite by modern feminism, we read in the collection's prologue that she first asks permission from her husband to speak. She does not conceal the patriarchal context in which she invents.

On the other hand, Hircan flatters his wife whose opinion he honors, and to whom he turns for her respected judgment when the group is deciding on how to entertain themselves. Nor is he in any way abashed to reveal his need for her sexual companionship. Later in the discussions, he explains their tardiness one morning by hinting that they were *pleasantly* detained. In the discussion following novella 40, we are told: *ceux qui estoient mariez ne dormirent pas si longtemps que les aultres. ("Married people do not sleep as much as others")* This is no marriage in name alone nor is the text's author interested only in what is going on in the minds of her characters.

Moreover, like any marriage, this one has its share of conflicts and disagreements. Throughout the exchanges, there are moments when husband and wife take quite opposite points of view on the story's meaning. He is decidedly a man of his times, less inclined to condemn extramarital delights than his wife, and unmistakably ready to uphold the sexual double standard. She, meanwhile, has strategies for ignoring his infidelities.

We see that Hircan is not above rudeness. At one point, he turns to Parlamente and says: *Taisez-vous* ("Be quiet") and she obeys. In brief, this marriage, like most then and perhaps like many now, was marked both by mutual respect and occasional disagreement.

Any study of the *Heptameron* must take into account not only the collection's plots but also all the sparkling and animated conversations that accompany them. Her anthology is at one and the same time a collection of stories and a social and psychological essay on sixteenth century French life.

In short, this is not only a storytelling session but also a kind of philosophical symposium where the exchange of views replicates many conversations in which the author had probably herself participated. Marguerite is intensely interested in the way these performers react to one another because she is a keen observer of the world which she inhabits. Her characters realistically bounce off each other's views.

She may not have invented the frame device, and indeed gives full credit to her predecessor, Boccaccio, for that. Nor did she invent the dialogue form. She had read both Plato and the Italian writer, Baldassare Castilgione. What she did invent was the unique concept of successfully linking the two together, true-to-life conversations to true-to-life storytelling. And for that, we must be eternally grateful.

III

Legacy

It isn't as if the Queen of Navarre received no recognition as a writer in her own lifetime. Many of her works circulated widely among friends. She was prone to entertain them with readings. Court ladies participated in productions of her plays. And at least one of her works, *Le Miroir de l'âme pécheresse,* enjoyed no less than eleven editions while Marguerite was still around to appreciate her success. But, with the exception of the *Heptameron,* by the end of the seventeenth century, most of her writings fell into near total oblivion; they seemed no longer to have any relevance for the wider reading public.

While her contemporaries Rabelais and Montaigne continued to be admired, Marguerite faded from sight. Were they better at what they did? Was she the victim of gender bias?

There is probably no simple answer to those questions.

But the undeniable fact remains that there has been a remarkable turnabout in our own age. As this is being written, two specialists are producing editions of Marguerite's complete opus, and her name pops up more and more frequently in specialist journals and at literary conferences. To what can we attribute this recovery of a nearly forgotten writer from the French Renaissance?

What, in short, does she have to say to twenty first century readers? She is, to be sure, a significant part of a phenomenon known as the Renaissance, and as such, crucially important to social historians. The Queen of

Navarre is something of a cultural barometer, and to leave her out of that history is to leave out a singularly critical part of the narrative.

But while Marguerite helps define an intellectual movement, she also brings to the whole issue a unique voice, the voice of a literary queen. That biographical fact in itself gives a different flavor to what she has to say. Through the prism of her specifically female vision, a woman who was at the very center of history, her words and ideas bring us a special perspective on the events of four hundred years ago.

Marguerite was not only an important historical figure; she was also a significant literary figure. We get two for the price of one: a conspicuous observer of the events of the day and a writer whose works tell us something about the intellectual tastes of the time. In brief, she is a *rara avis*: a literary queen.

Printed in Great Britain
by Amazon

32709870R00067